Give Me Lil

And Other Quotes From Great Ame

Give Me Liberty

And Other Quotes From Great American Leaders

Steven W. Allen

Award-winning author of *Founding Fathers – Uncommon Heroes*

Legal Awareness Series, Inc.
Mesa, Arizona

Published by Legal Awareness Series, Inc.
1550 E. McKellips Rd., Ste. 111
Mesa, AZ 85203

Printed in the United States of America

ISBN 1-879033-12-7

Warning — Disclaimer
The purpose of this book is to educate and entertain. The author or publisher does not guarantee that anyone following the techniques, suggestions, tips, ideas, quotes, or strategies will become successful. The author and publisher shall have neither liability or responsibility to anyone with respect to any loss or damage caused, or alleged to be caused, directly or indirectly by the information contained in this book.

Dedication

This book is dedicated to all the American citizens
who have pledged their lives for our freedom.
It is wonderful to live in a nation that supports our life,
liberty, and pursuit of happiness.

It is especially dedicated
to the Founders of this great nation.
They who fought to build our nation and fought for
the greatest cause ever . . . freedom.

FREE TO BE...

A life lived in liberty
is one I'm proud to live.
And shout alliance to the men
whose lives they did so give.

I see the blessings it brings to those
who live in this great land,
and name each one as men of grace
who brought freedom with their hand.

I see our flag wave bold and bright
and shine for all to see,
We pledge allegiance to the flag
that says we're "Free to be."

— Steven W. Allen

FREEDOM:

*The state of enjoying
civil and political liberty.*

The Boston Massacre had already taken American lives and King George continued to refuse to hear American petitions. Sarah Henry, the wife of Patrick Henry's youth, had died in February. Patrick Henry was a delegate to the Virginia Committee of Safety meeting to be held at St. John's Church in Richmond Virginia. Here he gave his immortal speech and he announced that the war for Liberty had already begun. Then he concluded with these words which keep his memory alive in the hearts of all Americans:

"Is life so dear, or peace so sweet, as to be purchased at the price of chains and slavery? Forbid it, Almighty God! Give me liberty, or give me death."

— Patrick Henry, March 23, 1775

"It is my full intention to devote my life and fortune in the cause we are engaged in, if need be."

— George Washington, three months before Adams
nominated him to become Commander-in-chief
of the united Colonial Army.

"We hold these truths to be self-evident: that all men are created equal; that they are endowed by their Creator with certain inalienable rights; that among these are life, liberty and the pursuit of happiness."

— Thomas Jefferson,
The Declaration of Independence,
July 4, 1776.

"They that can give up
an essential liberty to obtain
a little temporary safety,
deserve neither liberty nor safety."

— Benjamin Franklin, 1759

"Guard with jealous attention the public liberty. Suspect everyone who approaches that jewel. Unfortunately, nothing will preserve it but downright force. Whenever you give up that force, you are ruined."

— Patrick Henry

"The boisterous sea of liberty

is never without a wave."

— Thomas Jefferson

"To be prepared for war
is one of the most effectual means
of preserving the peace."

— George Washington

"Children should be educated
and instructed in the
principles of freedom."

— John Adams

"Liberty and Learning;
both best supported when
leaning each on the other."

— James Madison, Letter to W.T. Barry, August 4, 1822

"[We must] support every rational effort
to encourage schools, colleges,
universities, academies, and every
institution for propagating knowledge,
virtue, and religion among all people.
[It is] the only means
of preserving our constitution."

— John Adams, Inaugural Address, March 4, 1797

CHARACTER:

Moral excellence and firmness.

This entire chapter could have been filled with just the quotes of Benjamin Franklin. Some you may have heard already, some are fairly unknown. I included a few others for variety.

"The way to wealth…depends chiefly on two words, industry and frugality: that is, waste neither time nor money."

— Benjamin Franklin

"Early to bed, early to rise,
makes a man healthy,
wealthy, and wise."

— Benjamin Franklin

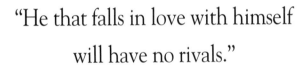

"He that falls in love with himself
will have no rivals."

— Benjamin Franklin

"Well done is better
than well said."

— Benjamin Franklin

> "A penny saved
>
> is a penny earned."
>
> — Benjamin Franklin

"In every nomination,
I have endeavored to make fitness
of character my primary object."

— George Washington

"…a perfect character might be
attended with the inconvenience of
being envied and hated;
and a benevolent man should allow
a few faults in himself, to keep his
friends in countenance."

— Benjamin Franklin

"If rascals knew the advantage of virtue, they would become honest men out of rascality."

— Benjamin Franklin

"To be true and just in all my dealings. To bear no malice nor hatred in my heart. To keep my hands from picking and stealing. Not to covet other men's goods; but to learn and labor truly, to get my own living, and to do my duty in that state of life unto which it shall please God to call me."

— Patrick Henry

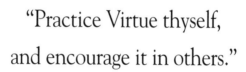

"Practice Virtue thyself,

and encourage it in others."

— Patrick Henry

"Whether this will prove a blessing
or a curse will depend on the use
our people will make of the blessings
which a gracious God hath
bestowed on us…
Righteousness alone can
exalt them as a nation."

— Patrick Henry

"If men were angels,

no government

would be necessary."

— James Madison

"Determine never to be idle
…It is wonderful how much
may be done if we are
always doing."

— Thomas Jefferson

"Do not bite at the bait of pleasure
till you know there is
no hook beneath it."

— Thomas Jefferson

"I'm a great believer in luck,
and I find the harder I work
the more I have of it."

— Thomas Jefferson

"In matters of style,
swim with the current;
in matters of principle,
stand like a rock."

— Thomas Jefferson

"Never trouble another
for what you can do for yourself."

— Thomas Jefferson

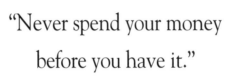

"Never spend your money

before you have it."

— Thomas Jefferson

"An honest man can feel

no pleasure in the exercise of power

over his fellow citizens."

— Thomas Jefferson,
letter to John Melish, January 13, 1813

"When angry, count ten,
before you speak;
if very angry, an hundred."

— Thomas Jefferson

"Whatever is begun in anger

ends in shame."

— Benjamin Franklin

"It is better to offer no excuse

than a bad one."

— George Washington,
letter to his niece Harriet Washington,
October 30, 1791

"Associate yourself with men
of good quality if you esteem
your own reputation for
'tis better to be alone
than in bad company."

— George Washington

"Labor to keep alive in your breast
that little spark of celestial fire
called conscience."

— George Washington

"Be courteous to all, but intimate with few, and let those few be well tried before you give them your confidence. True friendship is a plant of slow growth, and must undergo and withstand the shocks of adversity before it is entitled to the appellation."

— George Washington

"I hope I shall possess firmness and virtue enough to maintain what I consider the most enviable of all titles, the character of an honest man."

— George Washington

"The world is my country,
all mankind are my brethren,
and to do good is my religion."

— Thomas Paine

"The harder the conflict, the more glorious the triumph. What we obtain too cheap, we esteem too lightly; it is dearness only that gives everything its value. I love the man that can smile in trouble, that can gather strength from distress and grow brave by reflection."

— Thomas Paine

"'Tis the business of little minds
to shrink; but he whose heart is firm,
and whose conscience approves
his conduct, will pursue his
principles unto death."

— Thomas Paine

"Character is much easier

kept than recovered."

— Thomas Paine

"I will think ill of no man, not even in matters of truth; but rather excuse the faults I hear charged upon others, and upon proper occasion speak all the good I know of everybody."

— Benjamin Franklin (memorial program)

"If ignorance is bliss,

why aren't more people happy?"

— Thomas Jefferson

"The eternal difference between right and wrong does not fluctuate. It is immutable. And if the moral order does not change, then it imposes on us obligations toward God and man. Duty, then, requires the willingness to accept responsibility and to sacrifice one's desires to a higher law."

— Patrick Henry

"Three people can keep a secret
so long as two of them are dead."

— Benjamin Franklin

ACHIEVEMENT:

*A great or heroic deed
brought about by effort.*

"If you would not be forgotten
as soon as you are dead and rotten,
either write things worth reading
or do things worth the writing."

— Benjamin Franklin

"Nothing gives one person
so much advantage over another
as to remain always cool and unruffled
under all circumstances."

— Thomas Jefferson

"[Madison] acquired a habit of self-possession which placed at ready command the rich resources of his luminous and discriminating mind, and of his extensive information..."

— Thomas Jefferson,
speaking of James Madison

"Courage and perseverance
have a magical talisman,
before which difficulties disappear
and obstacles vanish into air."

— John Quincy Adams

"We have too many
high sounding words,
and too few actions
that correspond with them."

— Abigail Adams,
letter to John Adams, 1774

"Old minds are like old horses;

you must exercise them

if you wish to keep them

in working order."

— John Adams

"The real man smiles in trouble,
gathers strength from distress,
and grows brave by reflection."

— Thomas Paine

"A thing moderately good
is not so good as it ought to be.
Moderation in temper is always
a virtue, but moderation in
principle is always a vice."

— Thomas Paine,
The Rights of Man, 1792

"Be civil to all;

sociable to many;

familiar with few;

friend to one;

enemy to none."

— Benjamin Franklin

"There are three great friends:
an old wife, an old dog,
and ready money."

— Benjamin Franklin

"Lost time

is never found again."

— Benjamin Franklin

"I haven't failed,
I've found 10,000 ways
that don't work."

— Benjamin Franklin

GOVERNMENT:

*The act or process
of exercising control and
sovereign authority over.*

"The preservation of
the sacred fire of liberty
and the destiny of the republican
model of government are…
staked on the experiment
entrusted to the hands of
the American people."

— George Washington,
First Inaugural Address, April 30, 1789

"I hope ever to see
America among the foremost
nations of justice and liberality."

— George Washington

"Government is not reason,
it is not eloquence, it is force;
like fire, a troublesome servant
and a fearful master.
Never for a moment
should it be left
to irresponsible action."

— George Washington

"There is danger from all men. The only maxim of a free government ought to be to trust no man living with power to endanger the public liberty."

— John Adams,
Journal, 1772

"Of all the dispositions
and habits which lead to political
prosperity, religion and morality
are indispensable supports."

— George Washington in his Farewell Address,
September 17, 1796

"The aim of every political constitution is, or ought to be, first to obtain for rulers men who possess most wisdom to discern, and most virtue to pursue, the common good of the society; and…to take the most effectual precautions for keeping them virtuous whilst they continue to hold their public trust."

— James Madison

"He that would make his own liberty
secure must guard even his enemy
from oppression; for if he violates
this duty he establishes a precedent
that will reach to himself."

— Thomas Paine (1737–1809)

"Knowledge will forever govern
ignorance; and a people
who mean to be their own governours,
must arm themselves with the power
which knowledge gives."

— James Madison

"It cannot be emphasized too strongly or too often that this great nation was founded not by religionists but by Christians, not on religion but on the Gospel of Jesus Christ. We shall not fight alone. God presides over the destinies of nations."

— Patrick Henry, Virginia's first freely-elected
governor and founding father

HISTORY:

*A chronological record
of significant events.*

"We hold these truths to be sacred and undeniable; that all men are created equal and independent, that from that equal creation they derive rights inherent and inalienable, among which are the preservation of life, and liberty, and the pursuit of happiness."*

— Thomas Jefferson

*as originally written, compare this to the final
Declaration of Independence, as adopted by Congress.

SELF MASTERY:

*A display of great skill
at self-command.*

" Learning is not attained by chance,
it must be sought for with ardor
and attended to with diligence."

— Abigail Adams, 1780

"We are all born ignorant,
but one must work hard
to remain stupid."

— Benjamin Franklin

"We are not weak if we make a proper use of those means which the God of Nature has placed in our power…. The battle, sir, is not to the strong alone; it is to the vigilant, the active, the brave."

— Patrick Henry

"Remember not only to
say the right thing in the right place,
but far more difficult still, to leave
unsaid the wrong thing at the
tempting moment."

— Benjamin Franklin

"Do not anticipate trouble,
or worry about what may never
happen. Keep in the sunlight."

— Benjamin Franklin

"If you would persuade,
you must appeal to interest
rather than intellect."

— Benjamin Franklin

"To the generous mind
the heaviest debt is that
of gratitude, when it is not in
our power to repay it."

— Benjamin Franklin

"To lengthen thy Life,
lessen thy meals."

— Benjamin Franklin

"He that blows the coals
in quarrels that he has nothing
to do with, has no right to complain
if the sparks fly in his face."

— Benjamin Franklin

"He that has done you a kindness
will be more ready to do you another,
than he whom you yourself
have obliged."

— Benjamin Franklin

"There is no restraining

men's tongues or pens

when charged with a little vanity."

— George Washington

"By failing to prepare,

you are preparing to fail."

— Benjamin Franklin

"Nothing can stop the man
with the right mental attitude
from achieving this goal;
nothing on earth can help the man
with the wrong mental attitude."

— Thomas Jefferson

"Those who love deeply
never grow old; they may die
of old age, but they die young."

— Benjamin Franklin

"I will think ill of no man,
not even in matters of truth;
but rather excuse the faults I hear
charged upon others, and upon
proper occasion speak all the good
I know of everybody."

— Benjamin Franklin

"Our critics are our friends;
they show us our faults."

— Benjamin Franklin

"When you get to
the end of your rope,
tie a knot and hang on."

— Thomas Jefferson

FINANCE:

*The system that includes
the circulations of money,
the granting of credit, and the
making of investments.*

"Beware of little expenses;
a small leak will sink a great ship."

— Benjamin Franklin

"Few men have virtue
to withstand the highest bidder."

— George Washington

"He that is of the opinion
money will do everything
may well be suspected of doing
everything for money."

— Benjamin Franklin

"Drive thy business
or it will drive thee."

— Benjamin Franklin

"Creditors have
better memories
than debtors."

— Benjamin Franklin

"Necessity never made

a good bargain."

— Benjamin Franklin

"Having been poor is no shame,
but being ashamed of it, is."

— Benjamin Franklin

"Money never made a man happy yet, nor will it. There is nothing in its nature to produce happiness. The more a man has, the more he wants. Instead of its filling a vacuum, it makes one. If it satisfies one want, it doubles and trebles that want another way."

— Benjamin Franklin

"Think what you do
when you run into debt;
you give another power
over your liberty."

— Benjamin Franklin

"The glow of one warm thought
is to me worth more than money."

— Thomas Jefferson

"Wealth is not his that has it,

but his who enjoys it."

— Benjamin Franklin

"He does not possess wealth;
it possesses him."

— Benjamin Franklin

" Poverty often deprives a man
of all spirit and virtue.
It is hard for an empty bag
to stand upright."

— Benjamin Franklin

Free Patriotic E-Newsletter

Get Steven W. Allen's FREE Patriotic E-Newsletter

PATRIOTIC SALUTES

Sign up at *www.uncommonheroes.us*

You'll receive periodic information on:

- Little known stories about our Founding Fathers
- Leadership traits and application
- Patriotic and historical facts
- Holidays and proper flag flying
- And much more!

Also by Steven W. Allen

Founding Fathers — Uncommon Heroes
A book about the lives of our Founding Fathers: Benjamin Franklin, George Washington, Thomas Jefferson, John Adams, Patrick Henry, and James Madison. Learn fun and little known facts about their personalities, attitudes and even quirks. Finally, a history book that is fun to read.

**You Can't Take It With You,
So How are You Going to Leave it Behind?**
Estate planning attorney, Steven W. Allen, explores the differences between a Will and a Living Trust. Which one is right for you? An easy-to-understand review of each, clearly revealing which one will save you thousands of dollars.

For a complete catalog
of Steven W. Allen's books and resources, contact:

Publisher:
Legal Awareness Series, Inc.
(800)733-5297
info@legalawareness.com
www.legalawareness.com

Meet Steven W. Allen

At the age of 21, having been overseas for two years, Steven W. Allen returned home to the United States. What a wonderful feeling to return to America! It was then Steve began to feel an overwhelming sense of patriotism.

Now Steve inspires thousands of people by sharing stories from the lives of the founding fathers at universities and numerous civic and church groups. During the 14 years of these presentations, many attendees asked Steve where certain stories could be found. They requested he put these inspiring stories into a book to create one source of information.

And so Steve's book *Founding Fathers – Uncommon Heroes* was born. In his book, Steve gloriously brings to life the heroes of the American Revolution. During his research, Steve collected favorite quotes from his "heroes." And thus *Give Me Liberty* was created.

An Estate Planning Attorney by profession, Steve lives in Mesa, Arizona with his wife, where his patriotism has not dimmed. His clients comment on the "patriotic art exhibit" in the law office, where paintings and prints of the Founding Fathers and beginning America adorn the walls. His office also heralds a statue replica of George Washington, Benjamin Franklin, and Thomas Jefferson.

continued on next page

Steve received his Juris Doctor degree from Arizona State University college of law. He is a member of the State Bar of Arizona, The National Lawyers Association, The National Association of Elder Law Attorneys, and the National Speakers Association. Let him inspire your group with amazing stories and anecdotes from some of the founders of this great country, who pledged their life, liberty, and sacred honor for the noblest cause on earth...freedom.

Speaking Engagements

Steven W. Allen has delivered over 1,000 patriotic and motivational programs at conferences, civic groups and educational seminars nationwide and is available to speak for your event. He is the award winning author of *Founding Fathers — Uncommon Heroes*. By profession, Steve is an Estate Planning Attorney in Mesa, Arizona.

Speaking Topics:

Leadership
Founding Fathers, Patriotism
Personal Growth
Success
Motivation

Visit **www.steveallenspeaks.com** for more information
email: *steven@stevenallen.com*
phone: (800)733-5297

Quick Order Form

❏ *Founding Fathers — Uncommon Heroes* $19.95
(ISBN 1-879033-76-3)

❏*Give Me Liberty* $12.95
(ISBN 1-879033-11-9)

Name: _____

Address: _____

City, State, Zip: _____

Sales tax: Please add 7.8% for products shipped to Arizona
Shipping: U.S. add $4.00 for first book and $2.00 for each additional.
Call for international rates.

Payment: Make checks payable to: **Legal Awareness Series, Inc.**

Visa or Mastercard:

Card number: _____

Name on card: _____

Expiration date: _____

Send to:
Legal Awareness Series, Inc.
1550 E. McKellips Road, Suite 111
Mesa, Arizona 85203
Fax to: (480) 644-0072
Phone: 1-800-733-5297

Quick Order Form

❏ *Founding Fathers — Uncommon Heroes* $19.95
(ISBN 1-879033-76-3)

❏*Give Me Liberty* $12.95
(ISBN 1-879033-11-9)

Name: _____

Address: _____

City, State, Zip: _____

Sales tax: Please add 7.8% for products shipped to Arizona
Shipping: U.S. add $4.00 for first book and $2.00 for each additional.
Call for international rates.

Payment: Make checks payable to: **Legal Awareness Series, Inc.**

Visa or Mastercard:

Card number: _____

Name on card: _____

Expiration date: _____

Send to:
Legal Awareness Series, Inc.
1550 E. McKellips Road, Suite 111
Mesa, Arizona 85203
Fax to: (480) 644-0072
Phone: 1-800-733-5297